WALKS
IN

SWALEDALE

HILLSIDE GUIDES

LONG DISTANCE WALKS
- 1 • THE WESTMORLAND WAY
- 2 • THE FURNESS WAY
- 3 • THE CUMBERLAND WAY
- 7 • CLEVELAND WAY COMPANION
- 9 • THE NORTH BOWLAND TRAVERSE
  (by David Johnson)
- 16 • DALES WAY COMPANION
- 22 • THE COAST TO COAST WALK

CIRCULAR WALKS – YORKSHIRE DALES
- 4 • WALKS IN WHARFEDALE
- 5 • WALKS IN NIDDERDALE
- 6 • WALKS IN THE CRAVEN DALES
- 8 • WALKS IN WENSLEYDALE
- 10 • WALKS IN THREE PEAKS COUNTRY
- 11 • WALKS IN SWALEDALE
- 20 • RAMBLES IN WHARFEDALE
- 21 • WALKS ON THE HOWGILL FELLS

CIRCULAR WALKS – NORTH YORK MOORS
- 13 • WESTERN - Cleveland/Hambleton Hills
- 14 • SOUTHERN - Rosedale/Farndale/Bransdale
- 15 • NORTHERN - Eskdale and the Coast

CIRCULAR WALKS – SOUTH PENNINES
- 12 • WALKS IN BRONTE COUNTRY
- 17 • WALKS IN CALDERDALE

HILLWALKING – LAKE DISTRICT
- 18 • OVER LAKELAND MOUNTAINS
- 19 • OVER LAKELAND FELLS

FREEDOM OF THE DALES
40 selected walks
Full colour hardback

------

80 DALES WALKS
Omnibus edition of Books 4,6,8,11 and (in part)10,21
Published by Cordee, Leicester

WALKS
IN
SWALEDALE

by

Paul Hannon

HILLSIDE PUBLICATIONS

HILLSIDE PUBLICATIONS
11 Nessfield Grove
Exley Head
Keighley
West Yorkshire
BD22 6NU

First published 1987
5th (Revised) impression 1992

The maps in this book are based upon
the 1914-30 Ordnance Survey 1:10,560 (6") maps

Page 1 illustration: Calver Hill from Booze Moor

ISBN   1 870141 19 9

Printed in Great Britain by
Carnmor Print and Design
95/97 London Road
Preston
Lancashire
PR1 4BA

INTRODUCTION

The area explored in the pages of this guide is a very well defined one, being the valley of the river Swale from its beginnings in the tumbling becks of the wild Pennines to its departure from the Yorkshire Dales National Park near Richmond. Swaledale is the most northerly of Yorkshire's Dales and its remoteness from major centres of population has helped it remain relatively quiet and unchanged. Without insulting all of the other beautiful Dales valleys, it must be said that Swaledale is a little bit special.

Throughout its entire length the dale loses none of its grandeur, remaining steep-sided virtually all the way to Richmond. There is only one side-valley of any size, this being Arkengarthdale, the valley of Arkle Beck, which shares the characteristics of the main dale. With its colourful, sweeping fellsides, there is a strong hint of Lakeland in Swaledale.

This is walkers' territory *par excellence*, the dale's attractions being largely of the natural variety from heather moors to the waterfalls of Keld, and inevitably back to the swift-flowing and often tree-lined river. The Pennine Way crosses the valley head and the Coast to Coast Walk treats its followers to the entire length of the dale. There are two distinct types of walking in Swaledale, the lush meadows and the mining-ravaged hillsides. These two aspects of the dale are its very trademark. No other dale in the park has a riverbank which can be followed so closely for such a distance, and no other has such an intense concentration of remains of the lead mining industry. Every corner of the dale displays the evidence, from the mines on the moors down through the gills with their smelt mills to the villages with their miners' cottages. Many of the paths we follow lead up to the sites of former workings, which are slowly blending back into their hillsides. There is an impressiveness and even a certain beauty about these places which stem partly from an image of those hardy souls who, not that long ago, would walk several miles every day to slave away in these dark, damp holes.

The magnificent gateway to this glorious valley is Richmond, one of the finest little towns in the land. Its medieval charm and unrivalled character are a perfect match for the dale it guards. For those with transport it would make a reasonable base, but Reeth, the largest village, is far more satisfactorily situated in walking terms, with ample accommodation and several shops and inns.

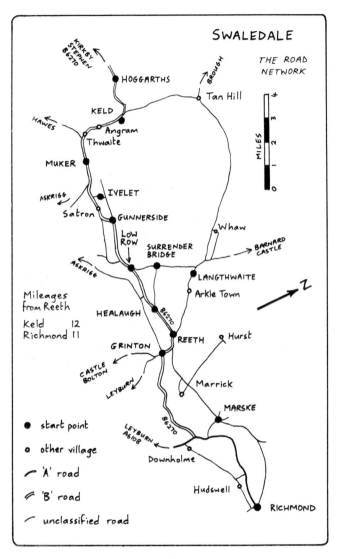

SWALEDALE

THE ROAD NETWORK

MILES

KIRKBY STEPHEN B6270

HOGGARTHS

BROUGH

Tan Hill

KELD

HAWES

Angram

Thwaite

MUKER

ASKRIGG

IVELET

Satron

GUNNERSIDE

Whaw

LOW ROW

SURRENDER BRIDGE

BARNARD CASTLE

ASKRIGG

LANGTHWAITE

Arkle Town

Mileages from Reeth

Keld   12
Richmond 11

HEALAUGH

B6270

REETH   Hurst

GRINTON

CASTLE BOLTON

LEYBURN

Marrick

MARSKE

LEYBURN A6108

B6270

Downholme

Hudswell

RICHMOND

● start point

○ other village

⌒ 'A' road

⫽ 'B' road

⌒ unclassified road

6

The 20 walks described range from 3½ to 11 miles in length, and the terrain similarly varies from riverside strolls to rather more strenuous moorland walking. All the walks are circular, and with an average distance of 5½ miles are ideally suited to half-day rambles.

Each walk is given its own chapter consisting of an 'immediate impression' diagram, detailed narrative and strip-map, and notes and illustrations of features of interest.

ORDNANCE SURVEY MAPS

While the strip-maps illustrating each walk should be sufficient to guide one safely around, they are unable to show the surrounding countryside. The remedy is an OS map.

1:50,000: Landranger sheets 92,98 and (for Walk 17 only) 99

1:25,000: Outdoor Leisure Map 30 - Yorkshire Dales North/Central (this covers all but Walk 20, which is on Pathfinder 609 - NZ10/SE19)

Ivelet Bridge

Overleaf are listed the various facilities which can be found in the area. Public transport takes the form of an infrequent bus service along the length of the valley from, inevitably, Richmond. Nearest rail stations are Darlington (for Richmond) or Kirkby Stephen (for the dalehead).

SOME USEFUL FACILITIES

	Accommodation	Inn	Car park	Bus service	Post Office	other shop	Payphone	WC
Angram				•			•	
Grinton	•	•		•	•		•	•
Gunnerside	•	•	•	•	•	•	•	•
Healaugh				•			•	
Hurst							•	
Ivelet							•	
Keld	•		•	•			•	•
Langthwaite	•	•			•	•	•	•
Low Row	•	•		•	•		•	•
Marrick	•						•	
Marske	•						•	
Muker	•	•	•	•	•	•	•	•
Reeth	•	•	•	•	•	•	•	•
Richmond	•	•	•	•	•	•	•	•
Satron	•			•			•	
Thwaite	•			•		•	•	

Please note: This is a general guide only

There is a reasonable spread of accommodation from hotels down the scale to youth hostels. These can be found at Keld and at Grinton. There is camping near Keld and Muker and at Reeth and Richmond.

SOME USEFUL ADDRESSES

Ramblers' Association
    1/5 Wandsworth Road, London SW8 2XX
        Tel. 071-582 6878

Youth Hostels Association
    Trevelyan House, St. Albans, Herts. AL1 2DY
        Tel. St. Albans (0727) 55215

Yorkshire Dales National Park Office
    Colvend, Hebden Road, Grassington,
    Skipton, North Yorkshire BD23 5LB
        Tel. Grassington (0756) 752748

Yorkshire and Humberside Tourist Board
    312 Tadcaster Road, York YO2 2HF
        Tel. York (0904) 707961

    Tourist Information -
        Reeth - Swaledale Folk Museum
            Tel. Richmond (0748) 84517
        Richmond - Friary Gardens
            Tel. Richmond (0748) 850252

Richmondshire Museum - Ryders Wynd, Richmond
        Tel. Richmond (0748) 825611

Georgian Theatre and Museum, Victoria Rd, Richmond
        Tel. Richmond (0748) 823021

Green Howards Regimental Museum
    Trinity Church, Market Place, Richmond
        Tel. Richmond (0748) 822133

United Automobile Services (buses)
    Grange Road, Darlington, Co. Durham
        Tel. Darlington (0325) 468771

Yorkshire Dales Society
    Otley Civic Centre, Cross Green, Otley LS21 1HD
        Tel. 0943 - 607868

THE WALKS

Listed below are the 20 walks described,
the number being the key to easy location

WALK	TITLE	MILES
1	THE CORPSE ROAD AND THE SWALE GORGE	6
2	FREMINGTON EDGE AND ARKLE BECK	$7\frac{3}{4}$
3	THE SWALE BELOW MUKER	$4\frac{3}{4}$
4	GREAT PINSEAT AND HARD LEVEL GILL	$5\frac{3}{4}$
5	THE BANKS OF THE SWALE	5
6	AROUND CALVER HILL	$6\frac{1}{4}$
7	MARSKE BECK AND SKELTON MOOR	$6\frac{1}{4}$
8	GUNNERSIDE GILL	6
9	COGDEN GILL AND GRINTON MOOR	4
10	AROUND KISDON HILL	$5\frac{1}{2}$
11	SLEI GILL AND BOOZE MOOR	$5\frac{3}{4}$
12	A CIRCUIT OF OXNOP GILL	$6\frac{1}{2}$
13	HARKERSIDE MOOR AND APEDALE	11
14	THE ENVIRONS OF LOW ROW	$3\frac{1}{2}$
15	MUKER SIDE AND THWAITE	$3\frac{1}{2}$
16	ARKENGARTHDALE	5
17	MARRICK PRIORY AND THE SWALE	6
18	BIRKDALE AND WHITSUNDALE	$5\frac{1}{2}$
19	THE ENVIRONS OF GUNNERSIDE	5
20	WHITCLIFFE SCAR AND THE SWALE	$7\frac{1}{2}$

THE WALKS

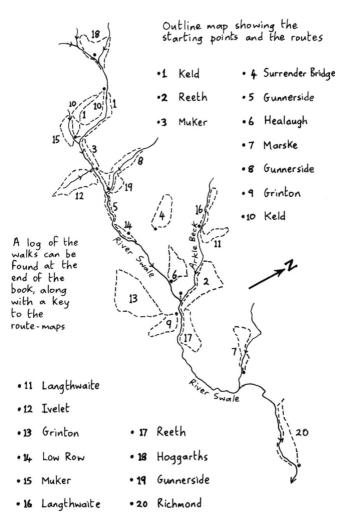

Outline map showing the
starting points and the routes

- 1 Keld
- 2 Reeth
- 3 Muker

- 4 Surrender Bridge
- 5 Gunnerside
- 6 Healaugh
- 7 Marske
- 8 Gunnerside
- 9 Grinton
- 10 Keld

A log of the walks can be found at the end of the book, along with a key to the route-maps

- 11 Langthwaite
- 12 Ivelet
- 13 Grinton
- 14 Low Row
- 15 Muker
- 16 Langthwaite

- 17 Reeth
- 18 Hoggarths
- 19 Gunnerside
- 20 Richmond

WALK 1

THE CORPSE ROAD AND THE SWALE GORGE

6 miles   *from Keld*

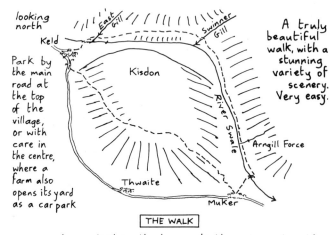

looking north

Keld

Park by the main road at the top of the village, or with care in the centre, where a farm also opens its yard as a car park

Kisdon

East Gill

Swinner Gill

River Swale

Arngill Force

Thwaite

Muker

A truly beautiful walk, with a stunning variety of scenery. Very easy.

THE WALK

     Leave Keld by the lane up to the main road, and turn left along it for a couple of minutes until a rough track drops down to the left. This is the old corpse road, which will lead unerringly over the hill to Muker. On crossing a tiny beck it begins to climb, soon easing out and passing through a couple of gates as it goes. Just beyond a short, walled section by some mining debris the summit of the track is reached, and a little down the other side the route of the Pennine Way is crossed as Kisdon Farm is seen across to the right. Continue down, briefly enclosed before joining the farm's access road. This well surfaced way takes us steeply down through the final two pastures to enter Muker along a short lane. Note the point of exit just to the left (signposted) on entering the village.

     On leaving Muker take the stile by a gate at the 'rear' of the village – as mentioned above – and a well-defined path crosses seven fields linked by solid stiles to arrive at the riverbank. Turn right to another stile to follow the Swale the few yards down to Ramps Holme Bridge. On the opposite bank drop down left to the river and soon a wide track is joined: it is accompanied almost all the way back to Keld. On crossing the first inflowing beck, be sure to stroll a short distance up its course to appreciate a charming waterfall.

Continuing by the river the track crosses a bridge below the ravine of Swinner Gill, then rises steeply before easing out above an increasingly impressive wooded, rocky gorge. This same track eventually descends to a farm bridge over East Gill - note the shared 'Pennine Way' and 'Coast to Coast' signpost - straight after which we take a left fork by East Gill Force to a footbridge over the Swale. From it take the path climbing right to a gate, and within minutes Keld is re-entered.

Lovely Seat
From Hooker
Mill Scar on
the Corpse Road

L Muker

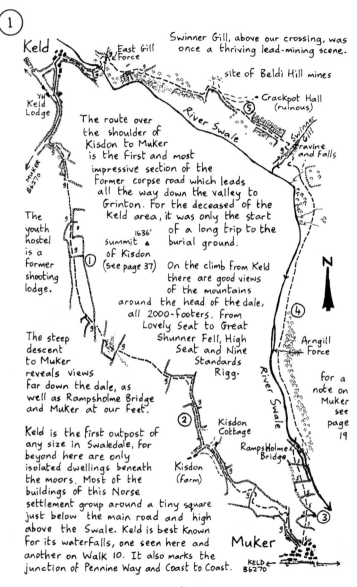

Keld

East Gill Force

Swinner Gill, above our crossing, was once a thriving lead-mining scene.

site of Beldi Hill mines

YH Keld Lodge

Crackpot Hall (ruinous)

⑤

River Swale

Swinner Gill

ravine and falls

MUKER B6270

The route over the shoulder of Kisdon to Muker is the first and most impressive section of the former corpse road which leads all the way down the valley to Grinton. For the deceased of the Keld area, it was only the start of a long trip to the burial ground.

1636' summit of Kisdon (see page 37)

The youth hostel is a former shooting lodge.

①

On the climb from Keld there are good views of the mountains around the head of the dale, all 2000-footers, from Lovely Seat to Great Shunner Fell, High Seat and Nine Standards Rigg.

N

④

Arngill Force

River Swale

The steep descent to Muker reveals views far down the dale, as well as Rampsholme Bridge and Muker at our feet.

for a note on Muker see page 19

Keld is the first outpost of any size in Swaledale, for beyond here are only isolated dwellings beneath the moors. Most of the buildings of this Norse settlement group around a tiny square just below the main road and high above the Swale. Keld is best known for its waterfalls, one seen here and another on Walk 10. It also marks the junction of Pennine Way and Coast to Coast.

②

Kisdon Cottage

Kisdon (farm)

Rampsholme Bridge

③

Muker

KELD← B6270

WALK 2

| FREMINGTON EDGE AND ARKLE BECK |

7¾ miles   from Reeth

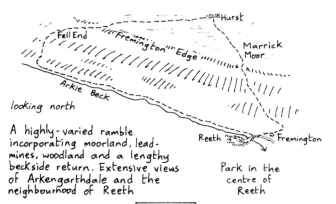

looking north

A highly-varied ramble
incorporating moorland, lead-
mines, woodland and a lengthy
beckside return. Extensive views
of Arkengarthdale and the
neighbourhood of Reeth

Park in the
centre of
Reeth

| THE WALK |

     Leave Reeth by the Richmond road, and immediately
after crossing the bridge over Arkle Beck take a stile on
the left. From another just across to the right go half-left
across the next field to a stile, then follow the right-hand
wall up to emerge onto a narrow lane in Fremington. Turn
almost at once up a walled track to the left to join another
lane and head to the left along it. Ignore a bridleway going
off, and begin the long climb to Fremington Edge.
     Remain on this lane throughout its course: at a
gate it begins to deteriorate into a rough track, passing near
the aptly named White House and continuing up to another
gate. Only a little more climbing and the top is gained. A
broad track heads away from a gate in the wall along the
top, bound unerringly across the moor for Hurst. It comes
into sight only on nearing it, and through a gate a prominent
old chimney is passed before reaching the hamlet.
     Turn left along its lane which ends before a pair
of gates back onto the moor. Yet another broad track heads
over it, taking us gradually up through a vast expanse of mining
debris back towards Fremington Edge. After passing through a
row of grouse butts the wall along the top appears: here leave
the track in favour of a gateway in a tiny angle of the wall.

With a slender trod to follow, head away to the scars of mining just ahead, keeping generally to their left. Continue on a virtually level course with two prominent cairns over to the left warning of broken cliffs, and North Rake Hush conspicuous directly ahead across the side valley of Slei Gill. As the gradient steepens bear round to the left away from a deep hush, dropping down to the foot of a mine-ravaged gully and thence down to a gate in the wall-corner below. From it descend by a wall to emerge onto a farm lane at Strothwaite Hall.

Go left along the lane to its demise at a farm, then cross two fields to Arkle Beck. Ignoring the footbridge take the gate ahead, after which our path breaks off the bridleway to remain nearer the beck. This it does for some time before being deflected away from a bend in it by way of yellow blobs of paint on numerous trees. From here on the way avoids the beck for some while, crossing the fields in a generally straight line to arrive at the prominent Castle Farm House.

From it our route heads away in the same direction, amidst as many collapsed walls as intact ones. Dropping to a long-abandoned farm the beck is rejoined, but within yards the path forks, and our choice is the track branching left. This soon passes through a gateway out of the trees and alongside a wall on the right. After two further gateways locate a stile on the right, descending past a barn to two slimline stiles in succession. Follow a wall to another stile and continue on through two more fields. The latter and lengthier of these returns us to the road at Reeth Bridge, graceful gateway to the village.

Reeth

GUNNERSIDE ↑ B6270

← LANGTHWAITE

Arkle Beck

Kiln ↑

note Kerbing on path by barn ←

Reeth Bridge

⑦

GRINTON B6270

→ Z

White House

①

High Fremington

For a note on Reeth see page 52

If you've enjoyed walking by the Arkle Beck, Walk 16 takes in a good deal more of it.

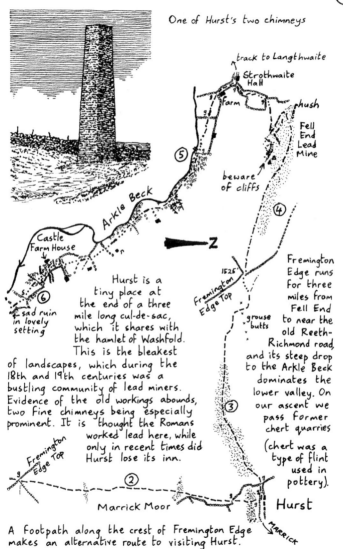

One of Hurst's two chimneys

track to Langthwaite

Strothwaite Hall

farm

phush

Fell End Lead Mine

⑤

Arkle Beck

beware of cliffs

④

Castle Farm House

⑥

sad ruin in lovely setting

Z

1525'

Fremington Edge Top

grouse butts

Fremington Edge runs for three miles from Fell End to near the old Reeth-Richmond road, and its steep drop to the Arkle Beck dominates the lower valley. On our ascent we pass former chert quarries

③

(chert was a type of flint used in pottery).

Hurst is a tiny place at the end of a three mile long cul-de-sac, which it shares with the hamlet of Washfold. This is the bleakest of landscapes, which during the 18th and 19th centuries was a bustling community of lead miners. Evidence of the old workings abounds, two fine chimneys being especially prominent. It is thought the Romans worked lead here, while only in recent times did Hurst lose its inn.

Fremington Edge Top

②

Marrick Moor

Hurst

MARRICK

A footpath along the crest of Fremington Edge makes an alternative route to visiting Hurst.

17

WALK 3   THE SWALE BELOW MUKER

4¾ miles   from Muker

looking north-west
Car park in the village
Ramps Holme Bridge
Calvert Houses
Muker
River Swale
Ivelet

Very easy walking
with good river scenery
and good views both up and down the dale

THE WALK

Leave Muker by a well-signposted stile by a gate between buildings at the 'rear' of the village, at the top of a short lane leading up to and behind the right of the post office. A well-defined path crosses seven fields linked by solid stiles to arrive at the riverbank. Turn right to another stile to follow the Swale downstream a few yards to Ramps Holme Bridge. Just upstream on the opposite bank a wide track is joined and then followed to the right. It climbs a little and soon receives a tarred surface, but remains unenclosed and traffic-free to run parallel with the river all the way to a junction at Gunnerside Lodge. Turn right to descend to Ivelet.

Continue down the lane from Ivelet to the river, and just along to the right is Ivelet Bridge. Do not cross it, however, but take a gate on the right to accompany the Swale upstream. The way is straightforward, with an intermittent path staying close to the river after an early detour from its bank. After a long mile the path cuts out a bend in the river by means of a line of obvious gap-stiles in parallel walls, then rejoins the Swale for the last five minutes to Ramps Holme Bridge. Re-cross it and retrace steps through the fields back to Muker.

Ramps Holme Bridge

Ramps Holme Bridge is a tall modern footbridge, and is the only crossing of the Swale between Keld and Ivelet Bridge. It is an excellent viewpoint for the lonely Swale gorge, as far upstream as the cleft of Swinner Gill.

The Farmers Arms, Muker

The path alongside the Swale witnesses some good river scenery as it flows over a wide, stony bed.

Muker is a good centre for the head of the dale, with accommodation, shops and an inn. The latter is the farthest up the valley, begging the pardon of Tan Hill, which at 1732 feet can in no way be said to be in a valley! Muker is probably the most picturesque village in the dale, with a fine grouping of buildings rising above the beck. The river Swale rejoins the main road just below the village, after their enforced split by Kisdon.

Prominent in most views is St. Mary's church, which was first built in 1580 to relieve Grinton's load, taking off its hands the upper dale which then made Muker an extensive parish, in areal extent at least. The present structure dates largely from 1890. Other interesting buildings are the Literary Institute of 1868, and the school, with tablets proclaiming that the famous Kearton brothers of Thwaite were former pupils. Muker is also the venue for the Swaledale Agricultural Show in September.

WALK 4

GREAT PINSEAT AND HARD LEVEL GILL

5¾ miles

from Surrender Bridge

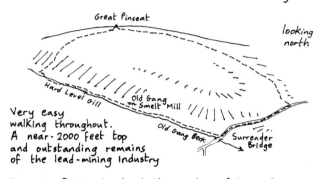

Great Pinseat

looking north

Hard Level Gill

Old Gang Smelt Mill

Old Gang Beck

Surrender Bridge

Very easy walking throughout. A near-2000 feet top and outstanding remains of the lead-mining industry

Surrender Bridge stands at the junction of two unfenced moor-roads, a mile north of Low Row, 2½ miles south of Langthwaite, and two miles west of Healaugh. It is named on O.S. 2½" maps but not on smaller scale maps. There are various parking spots.

THE WALK

From the bridge take the road climbing steeply east towards Langthwaite in Arkengarthdale. After the climb has subsided a broad track heads off to the left, and it leads unerringly and uneventfully up the moor. On levelling out Great Pinseat appears unspectacularly ahead, with a large sheepfold in front. Passing the fold, the track rises left to a pair of 'gateway' cairns amidst mining spoil.

Only a couple of minutes across to the right is the wall running along the top of Great Pinseat. The Ordnance Survey column on the summit is only seen if venturing across, for it hides immediately behind the wall. Do not cross the wall - it gains nothing but involves a double risk of damage: wild Stainmore to the north is just as bleak from our side!

Picking up the track at the next area of spoil (again cairned) the track - itself now cairned - descends through a band of mining debris to reach a gate. From it the track accompanies Flincher Gill downstream, crossing it twice before passing Level House Bridge. As Hard Level Gill and then Old Gang Beck it leads our track down through the Old Gang Smelt Mill and on for an eventual return to Surrender Bridge.

boundary stone

GREAT PINSEAT
0 1912'
O.S. column
54419

Flincher Gill

③

Great Pinseat, by virtue of its girth, gives views largely of moorland and old workings. High Dales summits on parade include Whernside, Great Coum, Lovely Seat, Great Shunner Fell and nearby Rogan's Seat.

A Reeth delivery van that lost its way has been nudged from its repose by the sheepfold into a large hole.

Fold

②

Wetshaw Bottom

↑ lives up to its name

← the sheepfold and the top appear

ruin

Level House Bridge

④

Hard Level Gill

active works

lagoon

Hard Level Force

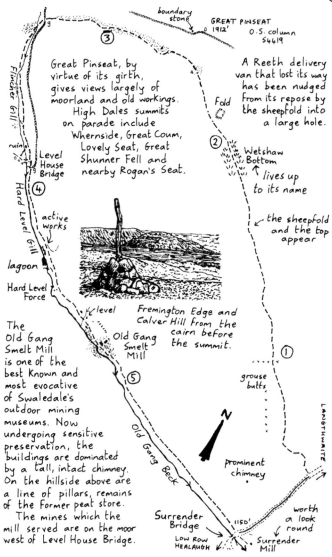

level

Old Gang Smelt Mill

⑤

Fremington Edge and Calver Hill from the cairn before the summit.

①

grouse butts

LANGTHWAITE

The Old Gang Smelt Mill is one of the best Known and most evocative of Swaledale's outdoor mining museums. Now undergoing sensitive preservation, the buildings are dominated by a tall, intact chimney. On the hillside above are a line of pillars, remains of the former peat store.

The mines which the mill served are on the moor west of Level House Bridge.

Old Gang Beck

N

prominent chimney

Surrender Bridge →

1150'

LOW ROW HEALAUGH ←

→ Surrender Mill

worth a look round

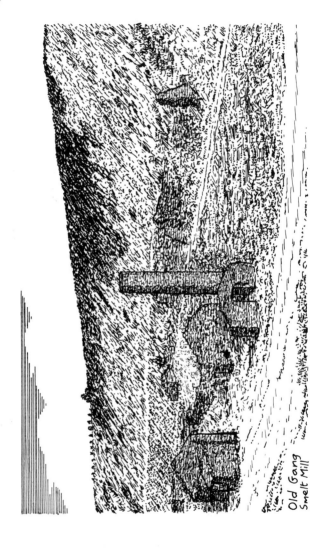

Old Gang
Smelt Mill

THE BANKS OF THE SWALE

from Gunnerside

5 miles

looking north

A simple, intimate riverside stroll

Parking area by bridge in village centre

THE WALK

Take the up-dale road out of the village to cross the bridge over the Swale, then leave it on the turn-off to Crackpot. This side road is quickly vacated after a cattle-grid in favour of a track to the left. This is Dubbing Garth Lane, which leads unfailingly down-river, generally sandwiched between a wall and the Swale itself. Eventually it becomes surfaced at a farm before reaching a T-junction. Turn left and soon left again to Isles Bridge.

Cross the bridge and use a stile on the left to commence the return, sticking with the river only until the first bend.

continued across

For a note on Gunnerside see page 31

As the river turns away an intermittent path strikes a direct course through the fields, a large pasture preceding two fences before arriving at a stile just before a crumbling barn. From it join the road as it approaches the returning Swale. As the road rises away rejoin the river's wooded bank, a path now clinging to it until forced back up onto the road at a steep, wooded bank.

This time the road is left at once, by a gate into a field. Drop steeply to regain the Swale's bank, which is followed pleasurably back to New Bridge. Just before Gunnerside Beck and the bridge, take a gate by a barn for a delightful finish by way of stiles and small fields back into the village.

23

WALK 6

6¼ miles

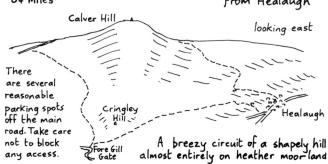

AROUND CALVER HILL

from Healaugh

Calver Hill

looking east

There are several reasonable parking spots off the main road. Take care not to block any access.

Cringley Hill

Fore Gill Gate

Healaugh

A breezy circuit of a shapely hill almost entirely on heather moorland

THE WALK

Leave the village by the up-dale Gunnerside road, and almost immediately turn right up a lesser road towards Kearton. This too is left at the first opportunity, up a drive to Thiernswood Hall. The track keeps left of the house to enter trees: at the end ignore the stile in front and take a gate on the right. In the wall-corner behind is a stile from where a track resumes to climb by the left-hand wall. Generally clear, it rises past the house at Nova Scotia to run below a walled enclosure to merge with another track. Now head up to the bottom side of another walled enclosure, and an improving path heads away from its far corner to pass above a fenced enclosure. Directly ahead the track reasserts itself while breasting the slope of Cringley Hill, and then remains clear to run undulatingly to arrive at the roadside at Fore Gill Gate.

Just before the gate, however, is a merging of tracks, and it is this other wide way we follow, now doubling back over the northern side of Cringley Hill. This infallible track eventually descends to join the road through Arkengarthdale. Turn right along its unfenced course for a good half-mile, then opposite a farm drive a footpath sign points us back onto the moor. A path rises to a prominent sheepfold: here turn left along a thin but generally clear path, which threads an enjoyable course through the heather. The way rises only imperceptibly as it remains below the markedly steeper upper slopes of Calver Hill.

Beyond a fenced enclosure beneath those aggressive slopes a length of wall is reached on the brow of Riddings Rigg. Head away in the same direction as before, a broadening way

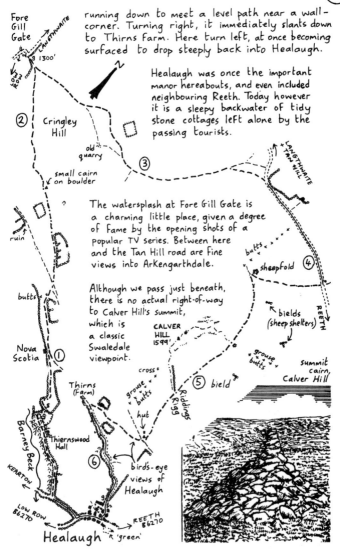

running down to meet a level path near a wall-corner. Turning right, it immediately slants down to Thirns farm. Here turn left, at once becoming surfaced to drop steeply back into Healaugh.

Healaugh was once the important manor hereabouts, and even included neighbouring Reeth. Today however it is a sleepy backwater of tidy stone cottages left alone by the passing tourists.

The watersplash at Fore Gill Gate is a charming little place, given a degree of fame by the opening shots of a popular TV series. Between here and the Tan Hill road are fine views into Arkengarthdale.

Although we pass just beneath, there is no actual right-of-way to Calver Hill's summit, which is a classic Swaledale viewpoint.

25

WALK 7
6¼ miles

MARSKE BECK AND SKELTON MOOR

From Marske

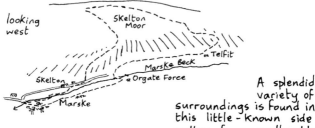

looking west

Skelton Moor

Telfit

Marske Beck

Orgate Force

Skelton

Marske

A splendid variety of surroundings is found in this little-known side valley, from woodland to moorland, and both of high quality

The best parking is just across the bridge from the village centre

THE WALK

From the spacious road junction above the church in the village centre, take the road branching off the 'through' road, and when it turns uphill continue on the level. Past a few cottages our way becomes a broad drive, and a charming woodland walk ensues. On eventual arrival at a fork, bear left on a woodland footpath where the main track keeps right to a gate. Continue on, emerging into the open to approach Orgate Farm. Just before the buildings turn down the concrete farm road to Marske Beck. A footbridge is provided next to the ford, and Orgate Force tumbles a little upstream.

Leave the beck by climbing the lane to a junction by a large barn, and turn right along the long farm drive to Telfit. Keep above the farm on a still-broad track scaling the hillside and doubling back to a gate. Rising by a wallside to a second gate, Skelton Moor is now gained. Go forward a few yards to a T-junction, and take the one straight ahead. It passes an old fold and then an Ordnance column atop the moor.

The track runs along to a gate into a lanehead, but instead of using it, turn sharp left on another track which links up with a wall to head back over the moor. Remain with the wall through a gate in an intervening wall, now joining a broader track with the valley and our outward route appearing far below. A splendid march to the next gate sees our track become enclosed to drop down onto a lane.

Turn briefly right to locate a stile on the left after a small barn. Head diagonally across the field to a stile from where a fence is followed away. When it turns left go straight on to drop to a substantial stone bridge just past an old waterwheel. Across the bridge, follow the beck downstream, using a gate into a brief wooded section to emerge at Marske Bridge.

Orgate Force

Marske Hall

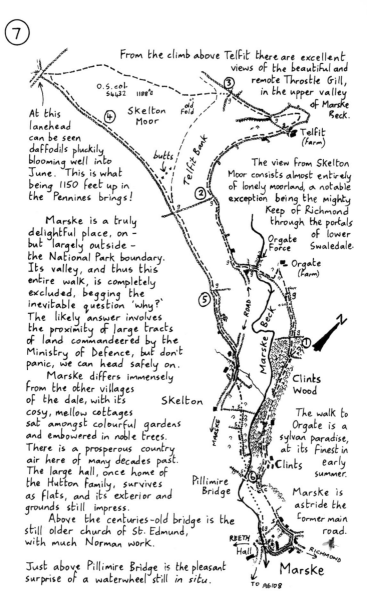

From the climb above Telfit there are excellent views of the beautiful and remote Throstle Gill, in the upper valley of Marske Beck.

O.S. col. 54432 1188'd

Skelton Moor

old Fold

At this lanehead can be seen daffodils pluckily blooming well into June. This is what being 1150 feet up in the Pennines brings!

butts

Telfit Bank

Telfit (farm)

The view from Skelton Moor consists almost entirely of lonely moorland, a notable exception being the mighty Keep of Richmond through the portals of lower Swaledale.

Orgate Force

Orgate (farm)

Marske is a truly delightful place, on - but largely outside - the National Park boundary. Its valley, and thus this entire walk, is completely excluded, begging the inevitable question 'why?' The likely answer involves the proximity of large tracts of land commandeered by the Ministry of Defence, but don't panic, we can head safely on.

Marske differs immensely from the other villages of the dale, with its cosy, mellow cottages sat amongst colourful gardens and embowered in noble trees. There is a prosperous country air here of many decades past. The large hall, once home of the Hutton family, survives as flats, and its exterior and grounds still impress.

Above the centuries-old bridge is the still older church of St. Edmund, with much Norman work.

Just above Pillimire Bridge is the pleasant surprise of a waterwheel still in situ.

Skelton

MARSKE

Pillimire Bridge

Marske Beck

ROAD

Clints Wood

The walk to Orgate is a sylvan paradise, at its finest in early summer.

Clints

Marske is astride the former main road.

REETH

Hall

RICHMOND

Marske

TO A6108

WALK 8

6 miles

GUNNERSIDE GILL

From Gunnerside

A fascinating exploration of this deeply-confined valley. The extensive remains of the lead-mines will stir the imagination. Overall, an absolute feast of colour.

Park in the village centre, by the bridge near the inn

looking west

THE WALK

Leave the bridge in the village centre by a wide track (on the inn-side of the bridge) following the beck upstream. After being deflected round Gunnerside Hall the beckside is rejoined and a path soon becomes clear to remain with it for some time. On entering thicker trees a stile admits to a long sliver of woodland from where we rise above the beck. The wood is left in impressive surrounds as we near Gunnerside Beck again, now running on through several stiles to arrive at the site of a crushing mill.

Keep left of the ruins along the flat pasture, and a path rises to reach- already- the final stiles of the walk. A wide, green path slants up the fellside above that last stile, soon levelling out to run parallel with the beck, now far below. An amazing scene of devastation soon greets the eyes as the extensive lead workings at Bunton are approached. Just beyond the last ruin in the immediate workings the path arrives at a crossroads: the left branch works its way down to the beck and then follows it up the gill floor to Blakethwaite Smelt Mill.

Amidst the ruins a large slab takes us over the beck, and any exploration might include a couple of hundred yards' detour on a path up the west bank of the beck for a closer look at Blakethwaite Force. Back at the smelt mill the return leg of the walk begins by crossing the inflowing Blind Gill, from where a superb green way rises gently back above the beck.

Avoid any deviations and continue to rise to the last mining remains of the day, where the track becomes level before it contours around Botcher Gill. Here we merge with a wide shooters' track, which beyond a gate commences a very gradual descent high above Gunnerside Gill.

When the track eventually curves sharply round to the right, leave it and bear left across the open pasture on a broad shoulder. Soon the rooftops of Gunnerside appear below. Now descend a little more steeply right to meet an unfenced road as it crosses a cattle-grid to enter the village.

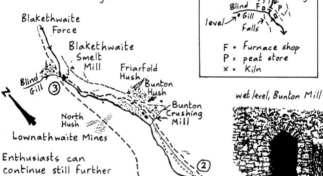

Enthusiasts can continue still further up the gill to reach the Blakethwaite lead mines and dams before returning to the smelt mill.

The lead mines are as much a part of Swaledale as the waterfalls of Keld, and Gunnerside Gill is an excellent venue for their inspection. At the terminus of the walk is the smelt mill serving the mines, which was built around 1820. Its best surviving feature is the peat store, whose ruinous form might be equally at home at Fountains Abbey. Two former crushing mills are visited, each with a long row of bunkers for storing the ore. There are also some classic hushes facing each other across the gill, and these were created by the release of previously dammed-up water which tore away the hillside in the search for new veins. The return path surveys all these features from a splendid, detached platform

Blakethwaite
Smelt Mill

Gunnerside, like most of its neighbours, had its heyday in lead mining times, when it was a busy centre for the once-thriving industry. Again in common with neighbouring villages it is now a sleepy place. It was founded by the Norsemen, and it would appear that Gunnar was a Viking chieftain : until recently the inn sported a superb pictorial sign depicting the said invader.

The village stands astride its own beck, which apart from a level quarter-mile from here to the Swale, spends all of its time tumbling down the deep gill immediately above the village. Gunnerside Gill, even without its open air lead mining 'museum', is arguably the most impressive in the Dales. For virtually four miles its steep sides sweep uninterruptedly down to the beck, with scale and colour of Lakeland proportions.

The mines, however, do add an extra element, and a gloomy day should be no deterrent to this walk. If anything, lingering cloud adds an almost tangible eeriness to the scene, assisted by the spirits of old miners, perhaps?

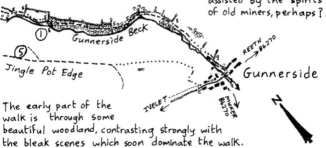

The early part of the walk is through some beautiful woodland, contrasting strongly with the bleak scenes which soon dominate the walk.

WALK 9

COGDEN GILL AND GRINTON MOOR

4 miles

from Grinton

Some steep gradients, but easy
route-finding and
worthy objectives

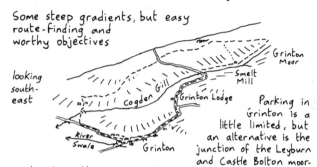

looking
south-
east

Parking in
Grinton is a
little limited, but
an alternative is the
junction of the Leyburn
and Castle Bolton moor-
roads above the village, just above the cattle-grid.

THE WALK

Leave Grinton by the lane climbing steeply from the angle of the main road by the inn. After emerging onto the open moor keep left at a fork, and the gradient finally fades as the youth hostel is passed. Within a further half-mile the road bends sharply to cross Cogden Gill. Take the track up the left bank to soon arrive at the remains of Grinton Smelt Mill.

After an inspection there is a choice of routes to the top of the highly conspicuous flue on the left. From the buildings there are tracks up either side of the beck. When the one on the opposite bank rejoins the main one, continue a little further to a minor brow roughly level with the top of the flue. Now turn sharp left to contour across the slope, possibly locating a very sketchy trod through the heather. The site of the former chimney at the flue top is soon reached. Anyone in a hurry could reach it even sooner by simply following the flue up from the mill to its very abrupt terminus.

From the flue top descend a few yards then swing round to the right below the crags of Sharrow Hill. A green track is joined which runs below the rocks then continues on to meet the moor-road to Leyburn. Cross straight over to a gate from where another pleasant track heads through two pastures before descending to Cogden Hall. Keeping to the left of most of the farm buildings and the hall, the access track is joined to debouch onto the Richmond road. Turn left for the final ten minutes back into Grinton.

Grinton, today a tiny village, was once the major centre for the dale above Richmond. A more curious feature is that it is the only settlement of any size on the south bank of the Swale. This no doubt stems from the south-facing slopes opposite seeing more of the sun. Grouped alongside the graceful bridge are the aptly-named inn and the church, which is known as the 'Cathedral of the Dales' because of its size. Until a chapel was established at Muker, Grinton parish was one of the largest in the land, extending westward through the entire valley as far as the Westmorland border.

As this was the only consecrated ground prior to 1580, the deceased of the upper dale had to be borne a long and arduous journey which we know today as the 'corpse road' (see Walk 1). The church itself is of Norman origin, but what we see is largely from the fifteenth century, being restored in the late nineteenth century.

Grinton is a good, honest Anglo-Saxon name, and nearby can be seen some of their strip lynchets, or cultivation terraces.

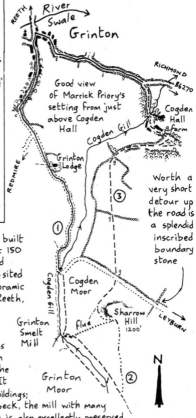

Good view of Marrick Priory's setting from just above Cogden Hall

Worth a very short detour up the road is a splendid inscribed boundary stone

Grinton Lodge was built as a shooting lodge about 150 years ago. This castellated building is now a superbly-sited youth hostel with a panoramic view across the dale to Reeth, Calver Hill, Arkengarthdale and Fremington Edge.

Grinton Smelt Mill was built early in the nineteenth century, and operated for the best part of that century. It boasts two well-preserved buildings; the peat store and, by the beck, the mill with many interesting features. The flue is also excellently preserved.

Grinton Lodge
Youth Hostel

The old flue,
Grinton
Smelt Mill

34

WALK 10

5½ miles

from Keld

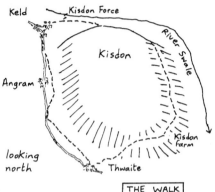

Keld — Kisdon Force

Kisdon

River Swale

Angram

Kisdon farm

looking north — Thwaite

A circumnavigation of a colourful little fell with excellent views on the return to Keld

Park by the main road at the top of the village, or with care in the centre, where a farm also opens its yard as a car park.

THE WALK

From the youth hostel head along the main road down the valley, and a little beyond a bridleway on the left a stile will be found. Here begins an invisible path through pleasant pastures, rendered easy to follow by punctuation by stiles at regular intervals. A good dozen are encountered, most being visible well in advance.

The road is rejoined after skirting the hamlet of Angram, and within a couple of minutes is vacated again at a stile on the left. Once more the path is but dots on the map, but the stiles again make life easy as we slope down to join a tiny beck. Thwaite is entered at the point where the Pennine Way departs it: after a look around and possibly a cuppa, return to this point. From here we trace the big daddy of the long distance paths back to Keld, and as a result the route-finding is made easy.

After two stiles our path strikes left through two fields to a bridge, then clings to the right of a field to climb to a stile at the top. A pleasant rise across a heathery slope ensues, continuing past a wall-corner to swing left up to another stile. Now with a wall on the left, go round to a gate, and then right alongside a wall to Kisdon farm.

Keep left of the farm to a gate, then take a walled track up to the left. When the wall parts company go straight ahead to join a track rising to the left. At a stile the way joins a near-level terrace which continues through many gateways and stiles and an occasional rash of stones. With trees now on the right and the path following the hillside round to the left, a gap in the accompanying wall is reached. Make use of it to descend to a junction of paths. Keld is but a few minutes along to the left, but for a short detour to see Kisdon Force, go to the right. Just down a slope is a gateway in the wall on the left, and from it a path goes down through the trees to a viewpoint for the waterfall. The descent to the very riverbank is somewhat steep.

To return to Keld rejoin the top path and go back along to the right, passing beneath tall cliffs before the way becomes enclosed to enter the village.

Kisdon Force

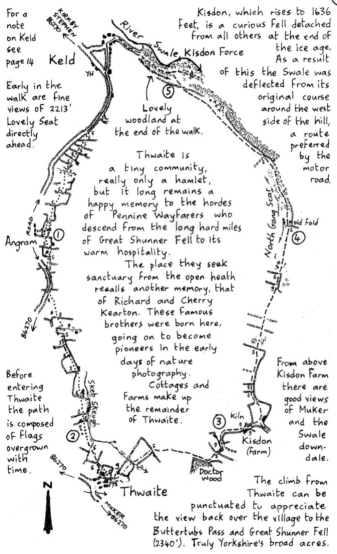

For a note on Keld see page 14

Keld

Early in the walk are fine views of 2213' Lovely Seat directly ahead.

KIRKBY STEPHEN ROAD

River Swale

YH

Kisdon Force

⑤

Lovely woodland at the end of the walk.

Kisdon, which rises to 1636 feet, is a curious fell detached from all others at the end of the ice age. As a result of this the Swale was deflected from its original course around the west side of the hill, a route preferred by the motor road.

Thwaite is a tiny community, really only a hamlet, but it long remains a happy memory to the hordes of Pennine Wayfarers who descend from the long hard miles of Great Shunner Fell to its warm hospitality.

The place they seek sanctuary from the open heath recalls another memory, that of Richard and Cherry Kearton. These famous brothers were born here, going on to become pioneers in the early days of nature photography.

Cottages and Farms make up the remainder of Thwaite.

North Gang Scar

old fold

④

Angram

ROAD

B6270

①

Before entering Thwaite the path is composed of flags overgrown with time.

B6270

Skeb Skeugh

②

N

MUKER B6270

Thwaite

Doctor Wood

③

kiln

Kisdon (farm)

From above Kisdon Farm there are good views of Muker and the Swale downdale.

The climb from Thwaite can be punctuated to appreciate the view back over the village to the Buttertubs Pass and Great Shunner Fell (2340'). Truly Yorkshire's broad acres.

WALK 11

SLEI GILL AND BOOZE MOOR

5¾ miles

from Langthwaite

A fine combination of beck and moorland surrounds

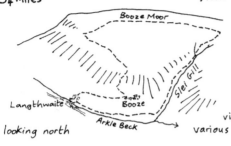

looking north

Parking can be found in the tiny village centre or various locations on the road just above

THE WALK

Cross the bridge into the heart of the village and turn right immediately behind the first house. A broad track accompanies Arkle Beck downstream before striking away from it into a wood. At a fork keep left, rising out of the trees to cross a field to a gate. Here leave the main track in favour of the grassy path continuing straight on. It crosses several enclosures alongside Slei Gill to arrive at the old lead workings, and continues rising as a superb green trod in the beck's company.

After a lengthy spell with the beck a gate admits to the open moor, and the path runs along to a stone arch amid more mining spoil. Here the beck divides and the path peters out: cross the left branch immediately above the arch, then head right to pick up the right (easterly) branch. A sketchy trod keeps above the little beck's marshy environs, and soon a line of shooting butts is reached. At the fourth one rise left to the beginnings of a prominent shooters' track: this climbs to a junction, whereupon go left to rise further to a crossroads. Our main track swings left, passing a shooting box and dividing for a while before arriving at a cairn overlooking Arkengarthdale. Further down is a junction above a wall: go left for a grand moorland crossing to another wall. Branch left to a corner and then drop to a stile in the lower corner (barn behind).

Having left the moor descend to a gate at the field-bottom and bear left on a path down between crumbling walls. Past a gate and a ruin we descend onto the lane in Booze. Turn left for a glimpse into its privacy, and then back to the right to return unfailingly - and finally steeply - into Langthwaite.

38

Fell End mines and Fremington Edge from Booze

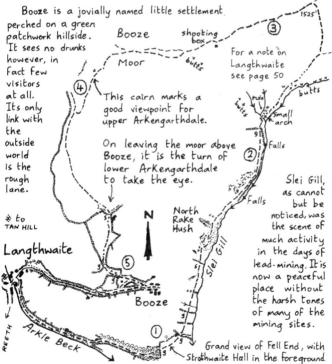

Booze is a jovially named little settlement, perched on a green patchwork hillside. It sees no drunks however, in fact few visitors at all. Its only link with the outside world is the rough lane.

Booze Moor

shooting box

butts

③ 1525'

For a note on Langthwaite see page 50

ruin

butts

butts

small arch

② Falls

This cairn marks a good viewpoint for upper Arkengarthdale.

④

On leaving the moor above Booze, it is the turn of lower Arkengarthdale to take the eye.

※ to TAN HILL

Langthwaite

⑤

N

Booze

North Rake Hush

Falls

Slei Gill

Slei Gill, as cannot but be noticed, was the scene of much activity in the days of lead-mining. It is now a peaceful place without the harsh tones of many of the mining sites.

REETH

Arkle Beck

①

Grand view of Fell End, with Strothwaite Hall in the foreground.

WALK 12

6½ miles

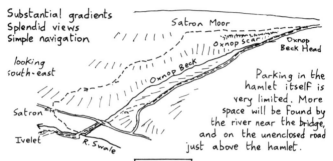

A CIRCUIT OF OXNOP GILL

from Ivelet

Substantial gradients
Splendid views
Simple navigation

looking south-east

Parking in the hamlet itself is very limited. More space will be found by the river near the bridge, and on the unenclosed road just above the hamlet.

THE WALK

From the houses at Ivelet descend the lane to the river and cross Ivelet Bridge, then take a stile on the left to accompany the Swale downstream. On nearing a wall bear right to a stile, from where a short, steep path leads up to another stile. The next stile is just left of the barn in front, then cross the field to one just right of a barn. One more field takes us to the hamlet of Satron, with a short snicket leading onto the road just to the right.

Cross straight over to a narrow byway which begins its steep pull immediately. This well-surfaced way is beneath our feet all the way to Oxnop Beck Head. At the several forks avoid the lesser branches right to farms: fortunately the steeper parts are out of the way fairly soon. Eventually it completely levels out to run above the rim of Oxnop Scar before merging into the Muker to Askrigg moorland road just short of its highest point.

Double back to the right along the road to commence the long descent. As far as the cattle grid a good deal of the walking can be enjoyed on the grassy verges. When the road becomes enclosed remain on it for a further three-quarters of a mile before taking a gate on the right marked by a footpath sign. Descend the field to a stile left of a wood, then round the next field-bottom keeping above the trees. When a farm comes into sight below, drop steeply right to a stile right of a barn. Two fields are now crossed to a stile alongside Oxnop Bridge. Cross the road bridge then turn down a narrow lane to return to Ivelet Bridge.

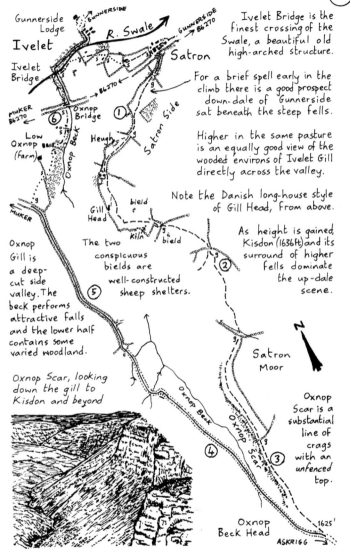

Ivelet Bridge is the finest crossing of the Swale, a beautiful old high-arched structure.

For a brief spell early in the climb there is a good prospect down-dale of Gunnerside sat beneath the steep fells.

Higher in the same pasture is an equally good view of the wooded environs of Ivelet Gill directly across the valley.

Note the Danish long-house style of Gill Head, from above.

As height is gained, Kisdon (1636ft) and its surround of higher fells dominate the up-dale scene.

The two conspicuous bields are well-constructed sheep shelters.

Oxnop Gill is a deep-cut side valley. The beck performs attractive falls and the lower half contains some varied woodland.

Oxnop Scar, looking down the gill to Kisdon and beyond

Oxnop Scar is a substantial line of crags with an unfenced top.

Map labels:

Gunnerside Lodge · Ivelet · Ivelet Bridge · MUKER B6270 · GUNNERSIDE · R. Swale · GUNNERSIDE B6270 · Satron · B6270 · Oxnop Bridge · Low Oxnop (farm) · Oxnop Beck · Heugh · Satron Side · MUKER · Gill Head · bield · Kiln · bield · Satron Moor · Oxnop Beck · Oxnop Scar · Oxnop Beck Head · 1625' · ASKRIGG → · N

(1) (2) (3) (4) (5) (6)

41

WALK 13   **HARKERSIDE MOOR AND APEDALE**

11 miles   *From Grinton*

looking
south-west

Apedale

Gibbon
Hill

Dent's
Houses

Greets
Hill

Harkerside
Moor

Grinton
Lodge

Grinton

A classic walk
on moorland throughout,
and easy to follow
virtually the whole way.
One for striding out and
blowing the cobwebs away.

Though mapped and measured from
the village centre, the best starting point
is the junction of roads from Castle Bolton and Leyburn
on the moor-edge above the village. There is a sizeable lay-by.
This walk is also ideal for sojourners at the superbly sited
Grinton Lodge youth hostel.

THE WALK

From the junction opt for the right-hand fork (to
Castle Bolton) and after a few minutes climbing, a bridlepath
strikes off to the right. Beyond a fence a beck is crossed and
the track rises slowly towards High Harker Hill. Briefly vague
in a grassy patch, it continues straight on, crossing another
wide track and rising to become clear again, and clearer still
on merging with another track. As a green strip it rises up
through highly conspicuous earthworks on the brow: from a
guidepost there head along to a cairn, and the track sets
off once more on a level course across the moor.

At an area of old lead workings cross to the far
side of them and then follow the track's sketchy green downhill
course alongside the remains. As the track winds down it soon
becomes clear again, swinging left to join a wider track before
arriving at a large shooting box. Go through the gateway by it
and maintain a level course on what is now a narrower footpath.
At a fork of thin green strips take the right one to the foot of

a magnificent limekiln just beyond. Climb the slope after it to join the higher path and resume a level course past a cairn.

The path now begins its only real sketchy spell with the most imperceptible of rises, passing above a prominent large cairn and bending round to the left. On welcome return to more heathery surroundings the path becomes clear with a conspicuous cairn on a brow a little ahead. From it the path continues to Birks Gill, rising past two grouse-butts before crossing above a tiny waterfall. Here the butts also cross the beck, but keep right of them and their peaty environs to rise to a large spoil heap.

A cairned track is followed left along a devastated strip to the moor-top. At the last cairn before the fence, bear right to a gateway with a large crater behind. From it a green track commences, first going left to another cairn then heading directly away from the fence. This is the head of Apedale, and the track is followed all the way down the valley to a crossroads of moorland tracks at Dent's Houses. Take the left arm which rises to Greets Hill, passing through an old fence on the top to commence what is positively the last leg of the journey.

The track descends away from the angle of fences, and on reaching lead mining remains it becomes unclear. Keep on the right side of the debris to join an unfenced moor-road. With its green verges it can be followed most pleasantly back down to the junction above Grinton, but a little alternative does exist: at the first bend go straight on down an almost hidden grass strip, crossing straight over a wide track and continuing down a path alongside grouse-butts to join another wide track. This is the one on which the walk began, and it soon rejoins the road just above the junction.

Greets Hill, looking across Apedale and Wensleydale to Penhill, Great Whernside and Buckden Pike

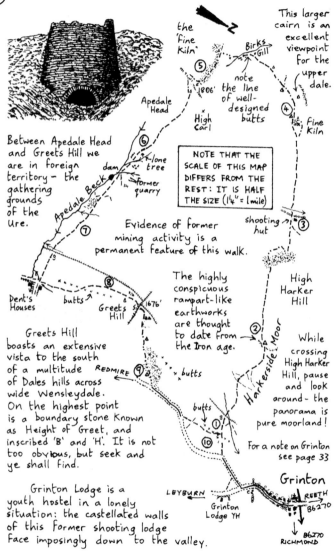

the 'Fine Kiln'

This larger cairn is an excellent viewpoint for the upper dale.

N

Birks Gill

⑤

1806'

note the line of well-designed butts

Apedale Head

④

Fine Kiln

High Carl ×

Between Apedale Head and Greets Hill we are in foreign territory - the gathering grounds of the Ure.

⑥

lone tree

dam

former quarry

Apedale Beck

NOTE THAT THE SCALE OF THIS MAP DIFFERS FROM THE REST: IT IS HALF THE SIZE (1¼" = 1 mile)

⑦

Evidence of former mining activity is a permanent feature of this walk.

shooting hut

③

Dent's Houses

⑧

butts

Greets Hill

1676'

The highly conspicuous rampart-like earthworks are thought to date from the Iron age.

②

High Harker Hill

Harkerside Moor

While crossing High Harker Hill, pause and look around - the panorama is pure moorland!

Greets Hill boasts an extensive vista to the south of a multitude of Dales hills across wide Wensleydale. On the highest point is a boundary stone known as Height of Greet, and inscribed 'B' and 'H'. It is not too obvious, but seek and ye shall find.

REDMIRE

⑨

butts

butts

①

⑩

For a note on Grinton see page 33

Grinton Lodge is a youth hostel in a lonely situation: the castellated walls of this former shooting lodge face imposingly down to the valley.

LEYBURN

Grinton Lodge YH

Grinton

REETH B6270

B6270 RICHMOND

WALK 14 | THE ENVIRONS OF LOW ROW

3½ miles   From Low Row!

The attractive surroundings of Low Row include
a superb riverside
ramble

looking north

Park on or
just off the
roadside
by the
church
and inn

THE WALK

From the inn head along the road to Reeth for ten
minutes or so, and at a wood on the right look for a footpath
sign to Isles Bridge. Here a path descends to the river and
follows it upstream, clinging to its bank the whole of the way
to Isles Bridge. Turn right up the road to a junction, and only
yards to the left climb an initially uninviting grass slope.

When the trees and brief path subside, go right
along the top of a wall and a path returns,
meeting a wider track which in turn joins
the road through Low Row.
Almost at once the road
can be avoided by using
the large expanse of
grass alongside. It must
finally be
rejoined at
the former
school opposite
the post office,
from where the
inn is only
minutes
further.

This section
of riverbank,
even by Swaledale
standards, is sheer
pleasure: virtually the
entire length is lined
with attractive trees.

Low Row straddles the
main valley road for a good
mile, and incorporates the twin
hamlet of Feetham, a name seldom
applied these days. A long open
'green' runs parallel with the road.
The focal point is where the church
and inn are sited. The latter is an
imposing structure dating from 1638.

WALK 15   MUKER SIDE AND THWAITE

3½ miles   From Muker

Good views from low slopes, and two lovely villages

looking
south

Muker / /
Side

Car park in the
village

Straw Beck

Muker

Usha
Gap

Thwaite

THE WALK

Cross the bridge at the east end of the village
and leave the road by an enclosed track rising slowly away
to the right. The track soon doubles back to climb towards
Muker Side. At a T-junction of walled tracks go right on a
level section, and at the next junction turn sharp right to
descend to a barn on a bend. Here vacate the imprisoning
walls by a gate on the left. Cross two field-bottoms on a track
passing an abandoned farm, and part way along the following
field take a gate in the wall to slope down a field to a
stile in the bottom-left corner. It leads to a footbridge after
which a track runs out onto the road.

If there is a reasonable amount of water in the
lively Cliff Beck under the footbridge, then a very short detour
is recommended. Take a stile just after the bridge and descend
the field to a stile onto the road at Scar Houses. Walk only
a few yards to the right to see a charming waterfall on the
same beck, just above the road. Retrace steps along the road to
meet the track and then continue past the Hawes junction
before dropping down into Thwaite.

Turn along the short lane in front of the shop,
and at the end a Pennine Way sign points the way through
a short ginnel and a couple of stiles into a field. Here the
Way strikes left, but we continue roughly parallel with a beck
on a sketchy path across four fields to reach a tiny bridge
over another beck coming in from the left. Cross the field-bottom
beyond, head past a barn to a stile from where a short enclosed
track joins the road at Usha Gap. Go left to the farm and up its
drive to a stile on the right. Cross to a stile near the far corner
of the field, from where a string of obvious stiles lead across a
host of field-bottoms to enter Muker just behind the inn.

Thwaite

For a note on Muker, see page 19
and for Thwaite, page 37

Thwaite

KELD B6270

Scar Houses

HAWES

Falls

B6270

Usha Gap (farm)

Usha Gap Bridge ③

Flagged path approaching Muker

Muker

Straw Beck

B6270 GUNNERSIDE

From the slopes of Muker Side Great Shunner Fell impresses straight ahead, while beyond Muker is the Swale Gorge backed by Rogan's Seat.

N

① Occupation Road

Three Loaning End

Muker Side

'loaning' means lane

WALK 16

5 miles

From Langthwaite

A valley walk with splendid
views of this relatively
little-known
side valley

looking north-east

Parking in the
village centre is limited,
but there are several other
places on the road above

THE WALK

Cross the bridge into the centre of the village, and leave by a short-lived lane on the left just after the shop. From a gate head across the field-bottom to a stile, then a sketchy path crosses two more fields to a house. Follow its drive down to join Scar House's wider drive, and head up it only a few yards to locate a path through the trees. It soon emerges and two field-bottoms precede a large pasture which is crossed parallel with the beck to a stile onto the Stang road.

Cross straight over and up the lane opposite: this quietest of byways is followed for a considerable time, soon becoming unenclosed. It is vacated after a mile and a half by a stile on the left shortly after a left fork near a group of modern barns, and just before another farm. Four fields are crossed in a direct descent before a super little path winds down through a colourful enclosure to enter Whaw.

Turn left to the bridge over Arkle Beck, without actually crossing it. From a gate on the left a farm track crosses three fields to approach the beck. A generally thin path now continues in fairly close company with the beck, enjoying one or two particularly attractive wooded moments. After a second series of stiles in quick succession a wooden footbridge is reached just one field short of the graceful arch of Eskeleth Bridge. Cross the footbridge and turn downstream to meet the road. Before taking the right-hand of two gates opposite, a short detour up the road is recommended to see a surviving powder house just over the wall on the right.

Back at the gate a drive heads away to become

enclosed at a junction: turn left a few yards and take a stile on the right opposite a house. A surfaced drive (the Scar House one again) is joined and followed along to the right to emerge onto the road adjacent to the church. A left turn - complete with footway - returns us through the rest of Langthwaite and back to the start.

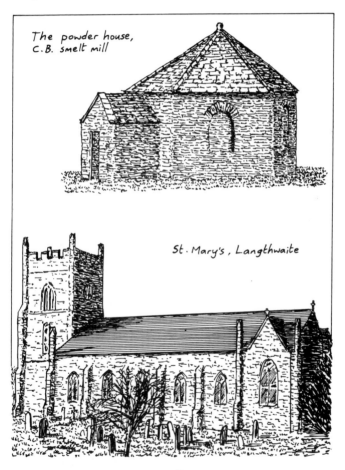

The powder house, C.B. smelt mill

St. Mary's, Langthwaite

Arkengarthdale is the Swale's major side-valley within the Dales, and the Arkle Beck is a tree-lined, fast-flowing tributary in keeping with its big brother. The beck rises on the bleak moors near the Tan Hill Inn, and takes its name from Arkle Town, a tiny settlement just south of Langthwaite.

Immense limekiln in excellent condition - a useful shelter if so required! Just before it can be seen a post inscribed 'NRYCC', recalling our famous Yorkshire 'Ridings'.

The peaceful road from High Eskeleth to Seal Houses is of sufficient altitude to give good views across the dale to the old workings of Whaw Moor and Great Punchard Gill.

A = former powder house

Scar House is probably the most up-market shooting lodge in the Dales.

Langthwaite is known as the capital of Arkengarthdale, but admittedly its rivals are few in number. This tiny village comprises of two distinct sections. Along the road through the dale are strewn a miscellany of buildings including the parish church of St. Mary, built in 1819 to serve the whole valley.

The other half of the village stands just below the road, a cluster of houses grouped on the east bank of the beck. This attractive scene will be instantly recognisable to devotees of the televised adventures of a certain veterinary surgeon. In amongst these buildings is one of Arkengarthdale's two hostelries, a cosy little place which has the appearance of a bookshop as much as an alehouse. The other inn is the 'C.B.' (named after a one-time local landowner, Charles Bathurst) which is on the road between the church and the Stang road.

Langthwaite was also the centre of the dale's lead mining industry.

WALK 17   **MARRICK PRIORY AND THE SWALE**

6 miles   *From Reeth*

Easy walking with good lower
valley scenery and surprise
distant views on the return

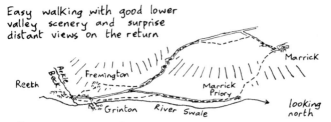

Park in the centre of Reeth

THE WALK

Leave Reeth by the Richmond road, and soon after
crossing the bridge over Arkle Beck take a wicket-gate on the
right. After leaving farm buildings behind, the path short-cuts
the beck's confluence with the Swale and bears to the left,
round a wall-corner to a wicket-gate and then straight ahead
to Grinton Bridge. Cross straight over the road, and a path
clings to the riverbank until forced by a wooded bank up onto
a fenced lane. Turn right along this quiet byway to Marrick
Priory, whose tower is in sight well in advance of reaching it.

Just after a cattle grid by the buildings, take a gate
on the left where a path rises to enter Steps Wood. A gem of
a flagged path climbs through it, and on leaving the trees
remain with the right-hand wall as a wide track materialises
to enter Marrick itself. At the first junction turn left up
onto the through road, and then go left along it past a
farm.

Shortly after a small dip in the road look out for a
stile on the left, and follow a wall away. At a stile cross to
the wall's other side and remain with it through a number of
intervening stiles to join the old Reeth-Richmond highway. A
steep descent of this now quiet lane ensues until just past a bend
by a drive to West Hag, a stile leads off to the right to begin
the last lap. This consists of an invisible field-path, which runs a
level course making use of various stiles and gateways.

Fremington is reached when a narrow, enclosed path is
joined just after crossing an enclosed green byway at right-angles.
Head along the footpath onto a narrow lane, following it left and

then right at the first opportunity. When it swings left to drop down steeply, go straight along a track to a stile. A path traces the left-hand wall through two further stiles, then crosses the fields with two final stiles preceding emergence back onto the road at Reeth Bridge.

Reeth is popularly known as the capital of upper Swaledale, in effect the whole of that part of the dale within the National Park boundary. It boasts an enviable position on the lower slopes of Calver Hill, well above the Swale and the Arkle Beck. It is actually the latter of these two watercourses to which it shows allegiance, with neighbouring Grinton claiming the Swale. The village centrepiece is a large, sloping green, with the main buildings stood back on all sides.

There is a confident air about this one-time market town which radiates chiefly from the hoary inns and the shops alongside the green. Reeth caters indiscriminately for dalesfolk and visitors alike, and is the ideal centre for a stay in the valley. Unfortunately parking limitations result in an untidy scene around the green in summer months. Inextricably linked with the lead mining days, Reeth was once much more populous. There is an absorbing folk museum here, while annual agricultural shows and festivals add to its local cultural attractions.

Fremington is a tiny but ancient Anglian settlement divided into two halves. Low Fremington stands astride the main road, while High Fremington is a haphazard grouping of dwellings with an enviable privacy linked by a network of narrow lanes and byways.

The Reeth area was a scene of sheer devastation in 1986 after an infamous hurricane passed this way.

For a note on Grinton see page 33

Marrick
Priory

The priory was founded in its pastoral riverside setting early in the 12th century for Benedictine nuns, and the greater part of the remains have been converted into a residential youth activity centre. Access is restricted to a gaze round the exterior. The adjacent farm has the name 'Abbey' Farm.

The village itself stands high above at a blustery thousand feet up. Today a sleepy backwater, it knew far busier times in the heyday of lead mining.

✳ The top of the road is an excellent viewpoint, the setting of Reeth under Calver Hill being particularly well displayed.

Also well seen on the descent is Grinton, with its isolated youth hostel at Grinton Lodge high on the moor above the village.

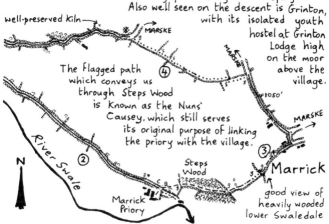

well-preserved kiln

MARSKE

The flagged path which conveys us through Steps Wood is known as the Nuns' Causey, which still serves its original purpose of linking the priory with the village.

1050'

MARSKE

River Swale

N

Steps Wood

Marrick Priory

Marrick

good view of heavily wooded lower Swaledale

WALK 18

5½ miles

BIRKDALE AND WHITSUNDALE

From Hoggarths

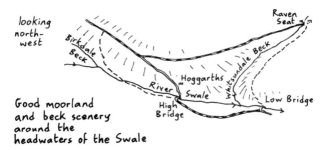

looking north-west

Good moorland and beck scenery around the headwaters of the Swale

The farm of Hoggarths is a good mile past the Tan Hill junction west of Keld. There is parking for several cars just after the road crosses the Swale before climbing to the farm.

THE WALK

From the Keld side of the bridge (High Bridge) take the track running upstream, and just through a gate fork to the left between a stream and a wall. At a barn take a gate to its right and continue on a level course, soon leaving a wall behind and joining the beckside. Follow it to a stone arched bridge and then resume up the opposite bank. After having been deflected by trees up to a gate, go on to join a track at an assortment of buildings at Firs.

Take the track to maintain our upstream course, but when it swings left to become enclosed, continue along another track alongside the left-hand wall. It soon rises above the wall to suddenly end: bear left, nearing the wall again to a stile at the far end. From it climb half-right to an old cottage, and then follow its access track up to a gate. Once through, leave the track and accompany the wall to the left. A little up to the right is the unfenced B6270 road, and when the wall nears it climb to join it in the vicinity of a footpath sign.

Now turn right along the road - or its attendant verge - and within a few minutes a minor junction is reached. Here turn left along the peaceful and largely unfenced access road to its destination and terminus, Raven Seat. Enter the hamlet by a stone arched bridge then turn right up into a farmyard. Take a gate in the right-hand wall and then head downstream, parallel with Whitsundale Beck through several fields.

From a gate just beyond an attractive waterfall, climb half-left to a barn, continuing on a now-level course through several more pastures. Beyond a gate in a fence the path forks: take the right one to pass along the bottom side of a large crumbling enclosure. At a guidepost beyond continue on a level sheeptrod to avoid wet ground by the barns below, then descend to a gate at the next wall junction. A good track then drops down past a Farm and over the Swale at Low Bridge to rejoin the B6270 Keld-Kirkby Stephen road.

Now turn right for a steady ten minutes along the road back to the next bridge, which is where the walk began.

Raven Seat is a tiny farming hamlet more than a little off the beaten track.

Unfortunately there is no public right-of-way to lonely Birkdale Tarn just above the road.

From the path one can gaze down into the deep wooded gorge of Oven Mouth.

The River Swale is formed by the meeting of Birkdale Beck and Great Sleddale Beck, and consequently our First mile is also the first mile of the Swale.

Whitsundale Beck is the first major tributary, the confluence being seen to good advantage from the road above, just before the walk ends.

Raven Seat

KIRKBY STEPHEN B6270

B

1525' Hill Top

B = Birkdale (derelict)

B6270

Firs

River Swale

Stone House

Hoggarths

Birkdale

High Bridge

falls

Whitsundale Beck

How Edge Scars

Oven Mouth

Eddy Fold

Smithy Holme

R. Swale

Low Bridge

KELD B6270

fg fold

falls

55

WALK 19

THE ENVIRONS OF GUNNERSIDE

5 miles   from Gunnerside

A walk of immense variety: lush meadows, high tracks
and lead-mining remains.
Marvellous views of
the main valley and
Gunnerside Gill

looking
north-west

Park in
the village
centre

THE WALK

From the bridge in the village centre, depart along the
lane to the right of the main up-dale road: it is identifiable by
the tidy little green at the start of it. The lane soon ends at
the school, and a gate to its right leads between modern housing
to a gate into a field. The way now heads across countless meadows
keeping generally level to arrive at a beck, crossing it by a tiny
footbridge to emerge into the hamlet of Ivelet.

At the lane turn up to the right, bearing right at
a junction, crossing a bridge and finally becoming level at the
open hillside. After a short while take a wide track branching up
to the left. It rises around the hill high above Gunnerside Gill,
and though it can be seen climbing far ahead, we leave it at the
first opportunity when a lesser track forks right to slope steadily
down to the beck. On the opposite bank are the remains of lead
workings, and a little further upstream cross the beck at a still-
tall ruin on our bank. Just behind a smaller ruin over the beck,
the main path up the gill is joined at a stile.

From the stile the path rises away from the beck,
but before reaching a wall-corner turn right at a crossroads
to begin the return to Gunnerside. The new path becomes sketchy
as it rises to a narrow stile below a low ruin. Continue across
the tops of two fields, emerging past a tiny section of wall and
on to a wall-corner. Keep well above the wall and a path appears
before joining a wide green track.

After going through a gateway the track passes
several groups of farm buildings, and remains fairly level before
meeting another track at a gate on the right. With Gunnerside far
below, go through the gate and accompany this gentle byway on
its steep but highly enjoyable descent back into the village.

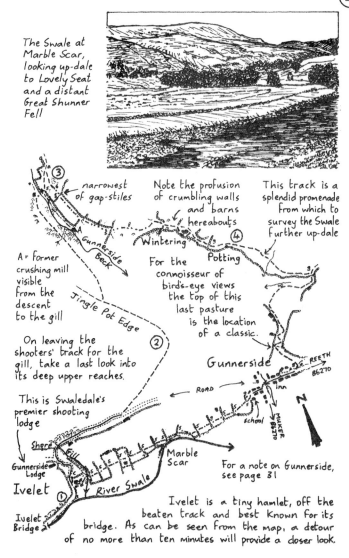

The Swale at Marble Scar, looking up-dale to Lovely Seat and a distant Great Shunner Fell

narrowest of gap-stiles

A = former crushing mill visible from the descent to the gill

Note the profusion of crumbling walls and barns hereabouts

Wintering Potting

This track is a splendid promenade from which to survey the Swale further up-dale

For the connoisseur of bird's-eye views the top of this last pasture is the location of a classic.

Gunnerside Beck

Jingle Pot Edge

On leaving the shooters' track for the gill, take a last look into its deep upper reaches.

This is Swaledale's premier shooting lodge

Gunnerside

REETH B6270

ROAD

inn

school

MUKER B6270

N

Shore

Gunnerside Lodge

Ivelet

Marble Scar

For a note on Gunnerside, see page 31

Ivelet Bridge

River Swale

Ivelet is a tiny hamlet, off the beaten track and best known for its bridge. As can be seen from the map, a detour of no more than ten minutes will provide a closer look.

57

WALK 20

WHITCLIFFE SCAR AND THE SWALE

7½ miles

from Richmond

looking north

Whitcliffe Scar

Deepdale

Applegarth

Richmond

River Swale

An airy promenade and riverside pastures provide scenery as varied as anywhere further up-dale

The centre of Richmond has ample car-parking

THE WALK

Leave the top end of the Market Place along Finkle Street, turning left along Newbiggin and right along Cravengate. A little further on the road swings left, and here leave it by a long avenue, Westfields, rising straight ahead. It leaves the houses to become a quiet lane, remaining surfaced until Whitcliffe Cottage. Now a track, remain on it until level with a farm on the left, and then climb half-right on a slender trod up to a brow. Bear left through a gateway, and then veer left to a fence running along the top of the eastern end of Whitcliffe Scar.

At an intervening wall we are conveyed to the scar side of the fence, and here we remain to reach the monument at Willance's Leap. Keep company with what is now a wall on the right, and our level path swings round with it, still above the Scar and then above a farm road in Deepdale. Eventually it is joined at its junction with a road, and we double back down the farm road as far as a cattle grid just short of High Applegarth. Take a stile just before it and descend by a well-collapsed wall, skirting the confines of Low Applegarth to a stile and gate in a fence. Just below it go left through a gateway, descending half-left through a gap in a wall, and similarly through a larger pasture to join a fence on the left. Passing a ruined barn continue down to a stile and thence onto the riverbank.

Two lengthy riverside pastures ensue, though in neither do we adhere to the Swale. The first is crossed on a sketchy way well to the left of the river, while in the second we abandon the riverbank half-way along, following a crumbling wall away to locate a stile into the trees. Now a clear path runs to the right

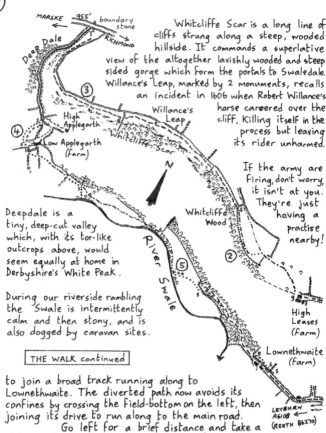

Whitcliffe Scar is a long line of cliffs strung along a steep, wooded hillside. It commands a superlative view of the altogether lavishly wooded and steep sided gorge which form the portals to Swaledale. Willance's Leap, marked by 2 monuments, recalls an incident in 1606 when Robert Willance's horse careered over the cliff, killing itself in the process but leaving its rider unharmed.

If the army are firing, don't worry, it isn't at you. They're just having a practise nearby!

Deepdale is a tiny, deep-cut valley which, with its tor-like outcrops above, would seem equally at home in Derbyshire's White Peak.

During our riverside rambling the Swale is intermittently calm and then stony, and is also dogged by caravan sites.

Map labels: MARSKE · 955' boundary stone · Deep Dale · RICHMOND · ③ · High Applegarth · ④ · Low Applegarth (Farm) · Willance's Leap · Whitcliffe Scar · N · Whitcliffe Wood · ② · River Swale · ⑤ · High Leases (Farm) · Lownethwaite (Farm) · LEYBURN A6108 (REETH B6270)

THE WALK continued

to join a broad track running along to Lownethwaite. The diverted path now avoids its confines by crossing the field-bottom on the left, then joining its drive to run along to the main road.

Go left for a brief distance and take a stile in the low wall opposite: a path descends to the river at a picnic site. Cross the footbridge high above the Swale and turn downstream. At the end of an avenue of trees the path bears right to a stile and runs below wooded cliffs (another path remains with the river). Another choice awaits further on as one branch climbs into the woods – a lovely walk – while the lower path continues on to the riverbank. Rough underfoot in parts, it is rejoined by the upper path for a splendid amble to Richmond Bridge. Cross it and rise straight up the road, taking a branch right to re-enter the Market Place.

Richmond is the gateway to Swaledale, although passing through it is the last thing to do. This is a truly remarkable town, steeped in history and retaining so much of its past, where other, less remote places have succumbed to the 20th century. Dominating the town is the castle, which stands on a rocky promontory high above the Swale. It was begun in 1071 by Alan Rufus, and the well-preserved ruins are now in the care of English Heritage and open to the public. Outstanding is the enormous 12th century keep, which watches over the whole town including, almost at its feet, the Market Place.

This equally-enormous feature shares double-bill with the castle, and has a multitude of uses. In the centre of its sloping cobbles is the church of the Holy Trinity with its 14th century tower. The building uniquely incorporates a row of shops, and houses the Green Howards Museum. Lined by shops and inns the Market Place is also used as a bus station as well as for its original purpose on Saturdays. A market cross is still very much in evidence.

Outside of the square, from which numerous wynds (narrow ways) radiate, is the parish church of St. Mary which includes a 14th century tower and 16th century stalls. Also in the vicinity is the impressively upstanding Grey Friars Tower, across the road from the Georgian Theatre. This fascinating place dates from 1788, and having been restored in the 1960s it now serves its original function once more.

The presence of the military around the town is due to the proximity of Catterick Camp. Also nearby are the Premonstratensian remains of Easby Abbey, dating from 1152.

Whitcliffe Cottage

①

If you've sampled this scenery on a good day, you may be surprised to discover you haven't set foot inside the National Park.

⑥

A6108

toilets

Westfields

River Swale

A6108

Richmond

Round Howe

The wooded eminence of Round Howe and much of the woodland in the vicinity is in the hands of the National Trust.

⑦

Huswell Woods

Castle

CATTERICK

→ DARLINGTON A6108

→ CATTERICK A6136

CATTERICK ↓

61

LOG OF THE WALKS

These two pages provide an opportunity to maintain a permanent record of the walks completed

WALK	DATE	TIME Start	TIME Finish	WEATHER	COMMENTS
1					
2					
3					
4					
5					
6					
7					
8					

9											
10											
11											
12											
13											
14											
15											
16											
17											
18											
19											
20											

KEY TO THE MAP SYMBOLS

Route   —·—·— clear   ·—··—··— sketchy   ··········· no path

Route on public road   wall   unenclosed   Fence/hedge

Abbreviations   g = gate   Railway line
s = stile   c = cattle grid

Buildings   Church   Cairns   summit   other   Limestone clints

Crags   Loose rock /scree   Marsh   Trees

river or beck   tarn or lake   bridge   waterfall

Miles from start   ③   Direction of North   N

Scale: approximately 2½ inches = 1 mile

THE COUNTRY CODE

- Respect the life and work of the countryside
- Protect wildlife, plants and trees
- Keep to public paths across farmland
- Safeguard water supplies
- Go carefully on country roads
- Keep dogs under control
- Guard against all risks of fire
- Fasten all gates
- Leave no litter- take it with you
- Make no unnecessary noise
- Leave livestock, crops and machinery alone
- Use gates and stiles to cross fences, hedges and walls